GO

BOWLS

THE GOLDEN RULES OF BOWLS

A CORGI BOOK 0 552 12601 2

First publication in Great Britain

PRINTING HISTORY
Corgi edition published 1985

Corgi Books are published by Transworld Publishers Ltd.,
Century House, 61-63 Uxbridge Road, Ealing, London W5 5SA,
in Australia by Transworld Publishers (Aust.) Pty. Ltd.,
26 Harley Crescent, Condell Park, NSW 2200, and in New
Zealand by Transworld Publishers (N.Z.) Ltd., Cnr. Moselle
and Waipareira Avenues, Henderson, Auckland.

Made and printed in Great Britain by
Hunt Barnard Printing Ltd., Aylesbury, Bucks.

The bowls must be of wood, rubber or composition and each set is required to carry an individual and distinguishing mark.

The Green shall form a square of not less than 33 yards and not more than 44 yards a side. It shall have a suitable playing surface which shall be level.

The Green shall be surrounded by a ditch.

Players, Umpires and Markers shall wear white, brown or black smooth-soled, heel-less footwear while playing on the Green or acting as Umpires or Markers.

Some Players find it beneficial to have two, three or even more sets of bowls.

When choosing bowls choose the heaviest you can manage comfortably.

The Player should be in good physical condition, especially when playing in a tournament or championship.

The serious Player should practise continuously in an endeavour to master all shots.

Always test the Green before beginning play.

Always maintain a good balance in the stance and throughout the movement of delivery.

To be valid the Jack must travel at least 25 yards from the mat.

A Player, at the moment of delivering the Jack or his bowl shall have one foot remaining entirely within the confines of the mat. The foot may be in contact with or over the mat.

A Player must decide on the length of time he stays on the mat. Too quick a delivery is careless and too long a wait may produce unwanted tension.

Only one bowl may be played at any one time.

On no account will a Player touch a bowl after it has come to rest and before the result of the end is known.

A Player must use the same hand throughout the game to deliver his bowls.

A Player should find a style of delivery that is legal and both comfortable and effective.

The Player should give total concentration to the game or match at all times.

Any leaf, paper or any other object may be moved by a Player if it interferes with his game.

The firing shot (or skittle or drive) is a shot delivered at speed down the Green and is a destructive shot if accurate.

When a Player has played before his turn, the opposing Skip shall have the right to stop the bowl in its course and it shall be played in its proper turn.

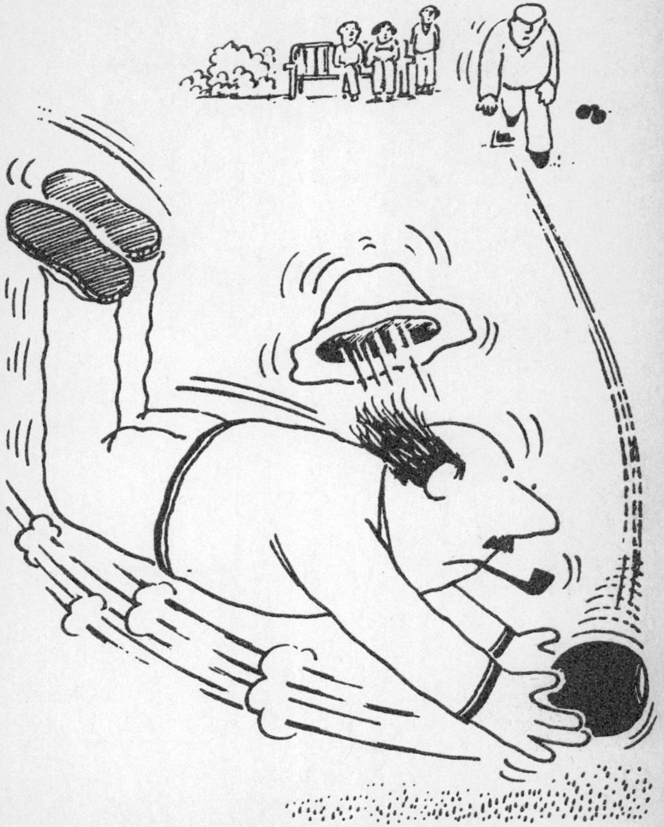

A good Skip must inspire confidence, drive and give encouragement to the other Players and remain calm under any kind of pressure.

The Skip shall have sole charge of his team and his instructions shall be observed by his Players. With the opposing Skip he shall decide all disputed points.

If during the course of play the position of the Jack or bowls be disturbed by wind, storm or any neutral object the end shall be declared 'dead' unless the Skips agree otherwise.

If a Player disturbs the Jack or a bowl the opposing Skip may have the bowl or Jack restored to its original position or accept the new position.

The Players playing shall not be interfered with, annoyed, or have their attention distracted in any way by their opponents.

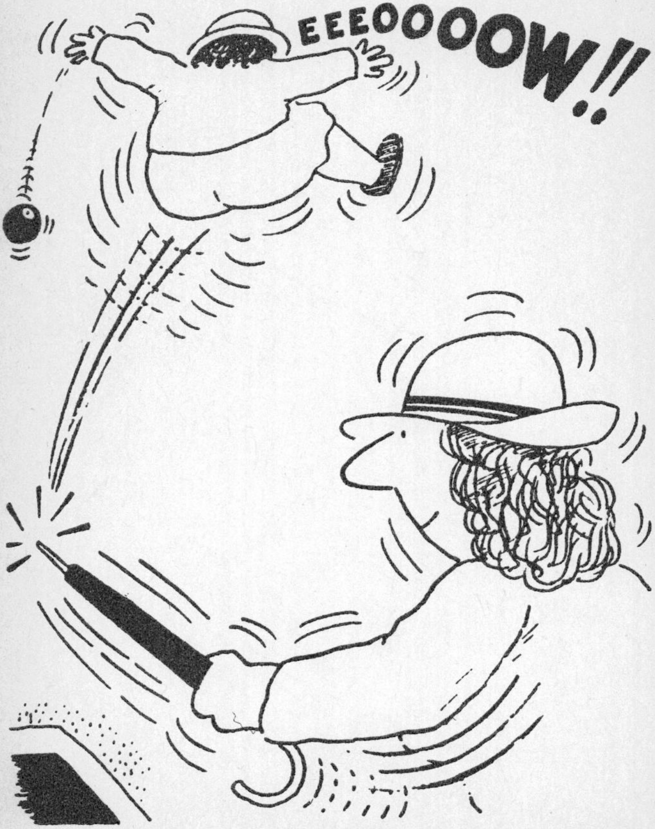

Under no circumstances shall any extraneous object to assist a Player be placed on the Green or on the Jack or on a bowl or elsewhere.

The Jack must be delivered with the same hand as the Player uses for delivering his bowls.

If a Crown Green game is interrupted (e.g. because of the weather) the position of the Jack is marked for the resumption of the end.

The Umpire shall determine whether a bowl has been properly delivered.

The Player must abide by the decision of the Umpire at all times.

When measuring a bowl which is resting on another, the Player, Marker or Umpire must use the best available means to secure it in its position before removing the other bowl.

The Umpire shall measure any shot or shots in dispute and for this purpose shall use a suitable measure. His decision shall be final.

The Umpire shall decide all questions as to the distance of the mat from the ditch and the Jack from the mat.

After appeal the Umpire shall decide whether bad light or any other valid reason shall stop play.

A Player may not impede the movement of an opponent's bowl which is in motion.

A Player may not delay play by leaving the rink except with the consent of his opponent and then not for more than ten minutes.

In match play, championships and tournaments it is compulsory to wear whites, which should be comfortable and not too tight fitting.

The Marker shall answer affirmatively or negatively a Player's enquiry as to whether a bowl is Jack high.

Only touchers (bowls which have touched the Jack in passing) rebounding from the face of the bank to the ditch or the rink shall remain in play.

On a wet, cold day the bowl may slip and the Player should counter this by the additional use of his or her thumb.

Betting or gambling in connection with any game shall not be permitted or engaged in within the grounds of any club.

It is an offence to commit ungentlemanly and unfair acts.

Persons not engaged in the game shall preserve an attitude of strict neutrality and neither by word or act disturb or advise the Players.

Remember to be courteous in defeat.

THE
END